THE LAST DAYS OF STEAM IN
BERKSHIRE

THE LAST DAYS OF STEAM IN
BERKSHIRE

– KEVIN ROBERTSON –

ALAN SUTTON
1987

ALAN SUTTON PUBLISHING
BRUNSWICK ROAD · GLOUCESTER

First published 1987

British Library Cataloguing in Publication Data

Robertson, Kevin
Last days of steam in Berkshire.
1. Great Western Railway — History
2. Locomotives — England — Berkshire — History
I. Title
385'36'1094229   HE3020.G8
ISBN 0-86299-395-4

*Endpapers: Front, 'Sir Edward Elgar' at the head of the London bound 'Cathedrals Express'
in Sonning Cutting east of Reading – Brian Davis
Back, 'Great Western' at the head of the London bound 'Cathedrals Express'
shown crossing the junction with the southern lines east of Reading – Brian Davis*

*Front Cover: No. 70024 'Vulcan' passing Tilehurst with the down
'Capitals United Express', 20.5.61. – Tony Molyneaux*

*Back Cover: Cross country steam, No. 2226 waiting to head north
from Compton on the D.N.&S. line – S.C. Townroe*

Typesetting and origination by
Alan Sutton Publishing Limited
Printed and bound in Great Britain by
Butler & Tanner Ltd, Frome and London

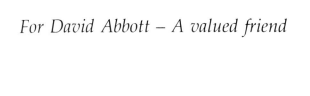

For David Abbott – A valued friend

Introduction

In presenting this the third album in *The Last Days of Steam* series I have once again embarked upon what is primarily a personal choice of photographs; yet it is one which I trust will have a wide ranging appeal.

Berkshire itself is perhaps a difficult county to portray with regard to its railways as, following boundary changes, Didcot and the lines to the west are now under the administrative control of Oxfordshire; although this was not the case during the period covered by the photographs. Again I have taken a liberal look at the county causing some slight duplication in areas associated with the previous volumes.

The photographs commence at Reading radiating out to the various main and branch lines. I hope most will be new to the reader as I am conscious that so often the same photograph is seen over and over again. Those that know me well will be aware I have a particular affinity for the D.N.& S. & Lambourn lines and so I make no excuses for including several photographs from these locations. These lines have a particular appeal simply because at a tender age I lived in a house backing onto the railway at Hermitage and was supposedly only quiet when a train went past the end of the garden . . . ! Later came hours spent by the lineside near Newbury Racecourse as a seemingly endless procession of 'Kings' and 'Castles' flashed through with sparkling paint, brass and copperwork glinting in the sunlight. My one regret is that I once turned down the opportunity of a trip on the Lambourn line and instead had to content myself with a walk over weed infested sleepers some years after closure.

In attempting to record the *Last Days of Steam in Berkshire* I have again been helped by many friends, old and new. Hugh Abbinnett, David Abbott, Brian Davis, Bob East of Newbury Station, John Fairman, Walter Gilburt and Tony Molyneaux all deserve a special mention for without their assistance none of this would have been possible.

Kevin Robertson

THE LAST DAYS OF STEAM IN
BERKSHIRE

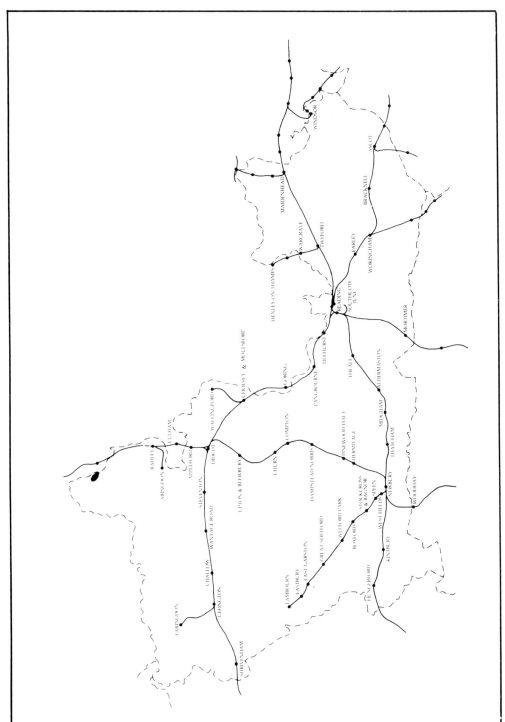

LAST DAYS OF STEAM IN BERKSHIRE

Only locations relevant to text are shown

Part 1: Reading to Maidenhead

Steam in Berkshire as it is probably best remembered. An immaculate 70xx series 'Castle', No. 7005 *Sir Edward Elgar* at the head of the London bound 'Cathedrals Express' in Sonning Cutting east of Reading.

Collection of Brian Davis

Without doubt the most important steam railway centre in Berkshire was Reading; indeed even today it remains the second busiest station on the Western Region after Paddington. Apart from the main line to Bristol the station is also the junction for the West of England line, normally referred to as the 'Berks and Hants', which from the vantage point of the former Reading West Main signalbox is seen curving away to the left. Crossing the maze of pointwork at the junction No. 6926 *Holkham Hall* slowly reverses towards the passenger station, a Southern Region 'Crompton' diesel can also be seen in the background.

Collection of Brian Davis

Viewed from ground level a railway engine can take on truly gargantuan proportions especially when compared with the human form. No. 6953 *Leighton Hall* allows the shunter to rest a moment as it moves past Reading West Junction.

Collection of Brian Davis

With a torrent of sulphorous fumes about to enter Reading West Main signalbox, No. 6153 takes the curve to Reading West at the head of a rake of Southern stock probably bound for Basingstoke. As if to confuse me 30 years after the photograph was taken, there was also a daily working of Southern coaches from Reading to Newbury so I have carefully avoided making too difinitive a statement! On the right the roadway led to Reading abbotoir and it was not unknown for animals to escape, running amok through the town before being recaptured.

Collection of Brian Davis

This was the interior of the West Main signalbox already mentioned in previous captions. The largest mechanical 'box on the 'Western and without doubt regarded as something of a showpiece. Manipulating its 200 plus levers were three men and a booking boy, the latter a form of apprenticeship into the grade of signalman. With at least four men visible and the hands of the clock showing 2.0 p.m. this may well have been change over time for the shift. The man at the levers is watching the progress of a train on the illuminated diagram above before he restores the lever in the frame. The lack of a duster when handling the levers is obvious and so indicating perhaps that this is a 'posed' view.

Collection of Brian Davis

No such pretensions here, with signal-man Ted Blackall for once not at work, instead being content to sit awhile. This is again the interior of West Main where Ted worked for some years having previously been at a number of other 'boxes in the area.

Collection of Brian Davis

The 61xx series of engines were a regular feature of the Berkshire scene being equally at home on freight or at the head of suburban passenger trains where they remained in service until ousted by the diesel multiple units. At the time this view was taken, No. 6161 was a Reading based engine and is seen here bound for Didcot at West Junction with a pick up goods about to take the crossover to the down relief line.

Collection of Brian Davis

Apart from its position on the main line to Bristol and the West, Reading was, and still is, an important meeting place for the routes from the Southern via both Redhill and Basingstoke. Accordingly, 'foreign' engine visitors especially from the Southern were common. SR 'U' class 2-6-0 No. 31631 opposite the cattle pens at the head of a freight bound for the Redhill line in June 1963.

Collection of Brian Davis

Another visitor from the Southern but this time bound for the Basingstoke branch. No. 32329 carried the name *Stephenson* and was originally built as a 4-6-4T before being rebuilt in this form in the 1930's. There were just seven members in the class, several of which were loaned to the GWR during the 1940's to assist in overcoming a temporary motive power shortfall. Later some of their duties were on the Reading–Southampton (via Basingstoke) trains, most of which were fairly light workings such as depicted here.

Collection of Brian Davis

It would be very tempting to produce an album of just 'three-quarter' views of trains, especially where they are as good as that seen here. I have tried however to provide a slightly more mixed viewpoint although I am sure no one will object too much to such a stunning view of No. 4077 *Chepstow Castle* as it leaves Reading with a Plymouth train comprising of 'chocolate and cream' liveried stock. This was one of the early batch of 'Castles' and is identified as such by the curved cover above the top of the inside cylinders. Even so it is paired with a later Hawksworth tender. *Chepstow Castle* was finally withdrawn in August 1962 after a working life of some 38½ years in which time it ran a total of 1.8 million miles.

Collection of Brian Davis

The effect of side lighting on a photograph is often dramatic and yet is difficult to capture to its best advantage. Here the photographer has achieved the desired effect, as watched by a single observer, No. 7006 *Lydford Castle* hurries through Reading non-stop on an express for Paddington. In the background the concrete tower is a renowned landmark of the town being part of the fire station in Caversham Road. 25.2.61.

Courtney Haydon

Awaiting the 'off' from the down main platform, No. 70025 *Western Star* draws admiring glances from a couple of small boys. At the time this was one of five 'Britannia' Pacifics allocated to the WR which were concentrated on Cardiff Canton shed.

Collection of Brian Davis

Reading has long been a favourite with rail enthusiasts, indeed even now a generation later it seems little has changed. The station staff gave up banning train spotters years before and instead erected a notice requesting all spotters to congregate at the same site at the west end of the up main platform. Neither were the 50 plus shown here an unusual number, with the majority paying little attention to the 'Warship' diesel! A point of interest is the bowler-hatted individual close by the cab of D818 *Glory*, who may well have been a locomotive inspector as such headgear was the recognised badge of office.

Collection of Brian Davis

In the days when porters were common a smart young member of staff directs a member of the public at Reading in 1955.

'R.A.' Collection

With the often fixed formation trains of today it is easy to forget the size of trains regularly hauled by steam engines. A good example is shown here, as No. 7024 *Powis Castle* enters the up main platform at the head of 12 bogie vehicles. 29.5.58.

Tony Molyneaux

The GWR and its successor the Western Region had a reputation for always doing things differently to everyone else! As one former Western man said '. . . the one thing wrong with nationalisation was that all the other railways were not absorbed by the GWR . . . !' Such an independant attitude was still prevalent some years after the advent of BR, with the Western Region inheriting the plans for two gas turbine machines the first of which was delivered in May 1950 and took the number 18000. Officially it was never named although a little unkindly it was sometimes dubbed *Kerosene Castle*. The engine is seen here on the up through road at Reading at the head of the 7.0 a.m. Weston-super-Mare to Paddington express in September 1955.

Len Davies

10

Another internal combustion engine vehicle and this time the original GWR diesel railcar, No. 1 of 1934. After a number of years on the Cardiff–Birmingham service several of this type of unit were transferred to the London division for use on the various branch line trains. No. 1 at Reading on 27.5.50 with a local bound for Henley which involved a reversal at Twyford.

W. Gilburt

No. 5012 *Berry Pomeroy Castle* starting off from Reading for Paddington with the 7.45 a.m. service from Worcester during 1950. The engine has the train reporting number '258' in chalk on the smokebox. On the tender the legend 'British Railways' is recorded in full and was a short-lived venture prior to the use of the 'cycling lion' emblem. As was usual for the period there is the informative station nameboard whilst at the platform behind is a mixed rake of 'MEX' or cattle wagons.

W. Gilburt

11

As well as the considerable procession of express passenger trains seen at the station, the Henley branch trains would sometimes reveal a 14xx on a single auto coach. Auto working was for years a feature so typical of the 'Western although it is perhaps best remembered on the various country branch lines of the West Country.

W. Gilburt

Another through goods working to the Southern and this time with 'U' class No. 31619 of Norwood Junction shed in charge. The train is on the goods avoiding lines at Reading which ran around the north of the passenger station. In the background the buildings are the old middle signal box and the new panel 'box respectively, with the vehicles on the extreme right on the spur that led down to the signal works. The diesel unit is in its original green livery and may well be a stopping service to Paddington. 25.1.64.

Courtney Haydon

Reading station was designed so that there were two through lines one between each pair of platforms. The line situated on the south side was almost exclusively used for non-stop trains for Paddington, while on the opposite side the through road was a useful stabling point for other traffic perhaps awaiting a clear signal through what was a heavily congested railway area. An example of the latter is shown here with one of the useful 22xx 'Collett Goods' No. 2210 at the head of an engineers' train in May 1960.

Tony Molyneaux

The few members of the 'Bulldog' class that survived into nationalised ownership spent their last days working a variety of goods services that clanked their way slowly between the various yards in the London division. From the crews' point of view such leisurely schedules were a blessing as the engine concerned would often be shy for steam and not at all comfortable to ride on. This is No. 3454 *Skylark*, one of the bird series of 'Bulldog' engines, at the head of a freight at Reading not long before withdrawal.

W. Gilburt

13

The more usual type of heavy freight locomotive in steam days, a 38xx series 2-8-0 but shown at the head of a parcels service at Reading in 1950. These engines together with the slightly earlier 28xx type were renowned for their brute strength. As more than one fireman put it, '. . . they would pull a house down'. More usually they ran the freight trains rather than parcels turns; although in emergencies on Summer Saturdays when everything that could move was being pressed into service some could even be found on expresses – I use the term loosely, passenger workings.

W. Gilburt

An early series Hall, No. 4923 *Evenley Hall* drawing into the up main platform at the head of a long train. It was said in steam days that there was hardly a passenger train in which two vehicles were alike – excusing of course such prestige workings as the 'Cornish Riviera' etc; and indeed here is a classic example with the front van not even of Western origin. The engine is coupled to what is termed an 'intermediate' tender a type which was used for a short time before the advent of the more usual high sided 4000 gallon variant. 23.4.50.

W. Gilburt

Next stop Twyford, then Maidenhead, Taplow and all stations to Paddington, for No. 6113 at the head of a long rake of stock. These engines had a remarkable turn of speed on such services and were usually well liked by their crews. The only disadvantage was that the footplate was rather cramped and hot during the summer, although this was a common problem with similar engines.

W. Gilburt

A wet April day in 1963 finds No. 6992 *Aborfield Hall* awaiting departure from Reading with the 11.15 a.m. Paddington to Hereford service. By this time steam was well and truly in decline, the generally shabby appearance heightened by the leaking steam.

Courtney Haydon

15

As referred to in my earlier book on Hampshire, I have always found night views of railways particularly attractive, although I have resisted the temptation to include more than one this time! Against a background of an almost deserted Reading station, Standard Class 4, No. 75068 waits in the bay after arrival on the 7.40 p.m. from Basingstoke in February 1962. This engine was one of a number in the class fitted with a double chimney and also a self-cleaning smokebox, the latter identified by the small 'SC' plate beneath the shed plate.

Courtney Haydon

A solemn crowd at a solemn moment, No. 34051 *Winston Churchill* at the head of the great man's funeral train passing through Reading on a grey January morning in 1965.

Collection of J. Fairman

At Reading in May 1965, on what was probably one of its last workings, a former bullion van, W819W, attached to a Hawksworth design coach. These vans, of which there were five to the basic design, were used solely for the transport of bullion from the ports to Paddington and the Bank of England. As a security measure several possessed doors on one side only and consequently care had to be exercised at the destination station to ensure that the doors were on the platform side. None of the type survived to be preserved.

Collection of J. Fairman

Reading, along with most major stations, had a pilot engine on duty for most of the day. Its function was twofold, to add and detach vehicles onto the main line services and also to act as a ready standby in the event of a locomotive failure. For this reason the pilot was usually a main line type of locomotive which, consequently appeared somewhat uncomfortable on shunting duties. On 29.7.58, No. 4092 *Dunraven Castle* was acting at pilot, caught here sandwiched between two vans and a parcels vehicle at the east end of the station.

Tony Molyneaux

Another view of the station pilot and once again a 'Castle', this time No. 4085 *Berkeley Castle*. Despite the 'British Railways' on the tender the engine has yet to receive its cast smokebox number and so identification from the front is via the none too clean set of numerals just visible on the buffer beam. Within Berkshire both Newbury and Didcot also possessed pilot engines.

W. Gilburt

A final view for the moment of Reading General – the suffix was added to avoid confusion with the West and Southern stations, with the station pilot on one of its usual duties. No. 6965 *Thirlestaine Hall* is seen pulling away westwards from the up main platform whilst a service for Paddington departs in the opposite direction. The 'Hall' had collected the two vans which were detached from the previous train. 23.4.50.

W. Gilburt

Transition from steam – a 'Hymek' diesel leaves Reading on the run to Paddington. The engine is in what was often regarded as the very attractive two tone green livery with white surrounds to the cab windows. The train behind is in all over maroon. This time the view is taken from Reading East Main signalbox and presents a panoramic view of the layout including in the background a 'Hall' 'Western diesel and 94xx pannier.

Collection of Brian Davis

Compared to the clean lines of so many of the Western steam classes, the Southern 'Q1' engines were nothing short of ugly, and yet such a dramatic difference gave them an appeal all of their own. The type were to be found within Berkshire primarily on the freights to and from the Southern Region via the Redhill line and would work as far as Scours Lane Yard before handing over to a WR machine. No. 33003 is shown crossing the Western main lines to take the Southern route just east of the station, with the fireman enjoying a breather before the long climb of the Southern route. Along with such trains the signals and that magnificent telegraph pole are now all memories.

Collection of Brian Davis

Old and new, and the steam engine *is* pulling the diesel not the other way round! A 'Hall', with a brand new diesel shunter in tow, heads east from Reading past Vastern Road goods depôt. The diesel was probably outward bound from Swindon, where it was built, to Acton or Old Oak for use and was coupled next to the steam engine officially so the crew could keep an eye on it during the journey. Although as one steam driver was heard to remark, '. . . as if we didn't have enough to do already . . .'.

Collection of Brian Davis

Officially to assess the merits of the various pre-nationalisation classes against each other, the new British Railways regime conducted a series of exchange trials during 1948 which involved running a number of 'foreign' engines on strange lines. One of these tests took a former LMS *Royal Scot* onto the Western Region where it was set to work on similar diagrams to the local 'Castle' and 'King' classes. One of these turns was on a Plymouth–Paddington express, via Westbury, and involved No. 46162 *Queens' Westminster Rifleman*. The train is shown shown leaving Reading on the last lap of the up journey to Paddington.

Collection of Brian Davis

At the same spot as the previous view, an immaculate 'Castle' at the head of the 'Cathedrals Express'. The engine is No. 7007 *Great Western*; a name given as it was the last of its type to be built at Swindon before nationalisation. Under BR former GWR engines had their painted front numbers replaced by a cast plate on the smokebox door, based on a former LMS practice. This was all very well until engines were working trains when reporting numbers were carried such as here, then the smokebox number became totally obscured, thus making identification difficult if not impossible.

Collection of Brian Davis

Away from trains, briefly, this time to the more mundane matter of track maintainance, always very important and yet often overlooked by traveller and enthusiast alike. This man is attending to a points heater which were intended to prevent frost and snow from interfering with the remote operation of the crossover. Unfortunately as many of us know this does not always work in practice . . . !

'R.A.' Collection

For some years three 'Hall' class engines were allocated to Didcot shed, one of which was No. 5935 *Norton Hall*. The engine is depicted on the up main line in Sonning Cutting with Class A, or express train headcodes in April 1956.

Collection of P.T. Earl.

Sonning Cutting again, a favourite with the photographer and with scenery like this it is easy to see why. No. 7021 *Haverfordwest Castle* at the head of the down 'Capitals United Express', 28.8.59.

Collection of Brian Davis

The express trains of today on the Western Region consist of either seven or eight coaches with a power unit at either end, a far cry from when a steam locomotive with less than half the power would tackle ten or more vehicles. Again in the sylvan setting of Sonning Cutting, No. 7031 *Cromwell's Castle* hurries a Worcester–Paddington express past a group of permanent way workers on a hot June day in 1963.

Collection of Brian Davis

East from Reading on the main line the first station was Twyford, which was also the junction for the Henley branch. No. 5062 *Earl of Shaftesbury* is about to disturb the peace for the Twyford West signalman as it heads for Paddington on a 13 coach working from South Wales, 10.4.54.

W. Gilburt

A final view of Sonning, this time at the east end, and perhaps fittingly, with No. 18000 again but now on a westbound train. Unusually the engine is only on a set of six coaches, five of which are brand new BR Mk. 1's, so this may well have been a special working. In service some men liked and others loathed this machine, for although it meant the fireman had little to do, the smell of kerosene both within and around it was ever present. This aroma even penetrated the following coaches and was another reason why the prototype was doomed to failure. Certainly power wise there seemed no limit to its output and it was more than equal to the largest steam design. The four tracks are, left to right, up relief, down relief, up main and down main, the Western keeping the routes separate compared with some other regions. Even today the same system persists, Western men still refering to 'relief' lines rather than the more widely adopted term 'slow'.

Len Davies

Apart from the fast passenger workings, the 'Castle's' were regularly used on the milk trains. In later years these were usually formed from fully fitted 6-wheeled tanks and so were able to run at faster speeds. The weight of these trains was another factor in using larger engines, together with the importance of ensuring that the milk reached the London dairies without delay. Accordingly, both the full London bound workings and the return empties were given priority, the latter to ensure that there was sufficient time for reloading at the various creameries in Wiltshire, Devon, Cornwall and Wales. In the spring of 1955, No. 7037 *Swindon*, the last 'Castle' class engine to be built, was in charge of one of the return empty trains, and is seen bursting under the overbridge at Twyford with its train of tanks rattling behind.

Collection of P.T. Earl

On the same day No. 5932 *Haydon Hall* was in charge of empty parcel vans on the up relief line, with the train itself made up of a motley selection of vehicles. Evidently the tender at least had not received a repaint for some time as it still sports evidence of private ownership more than six years after nationalisation 10.4.54.

W. Gilburt

A brief respite from the main line now and time for a glance at the Henley-on-Thames branch which was in Berkshire as far as the first station at Wargrave. The opening view shows 94xx No. 9403 just entering the bay at Twyford on a working from Henley. The engine would later run round before returning to the terminus. This working was performed by a Reading engine and crew, the lack of variety in just shuttling to and fro for most of the day meant it was not always the most popular turn.

W. Gilburt

During the morning and evening peak times there were commuter trains between Henley and Paddington, although outside these hours a single coach or two was sufficient to maintain the service. In this quite stunning view an early 57xx series pannier tank, No. 5766 runs quietly along south of Wargrave bound for Twyford on 22.9.51.

J.F. Russell Smith/National Railway Museum

The Henley branch was also worked by the diesel railcars for a while. No. 1 shown at Wargrave on the up service from Henley to Twyford during the early 1950's.

Lens of Sutton

Returning again to Twyford we find No. 2945 *Hillingdon Court* leaving Twyford for Paddington on a ten coach stopping train in May 1950. Originally employed on front line duties, the 'Saint' class engines were rapidly being withdrawn at this time although their direct desendants, the numerous 'Hall' class lasted until the very end of Western steam. First introduced in 1902 the 'Saint's' were very advanced for their time incorporating a number of features later included in the very last steam engines to run in regular service on BR

Collection of R. Sherlock

The concept of camping coaches was more usually associated with various rural lines in Wales and the West Country. Yet the two intermediate stations on the Henley branch, Wargrave and Shiplake, both possessed such vehicles for a number of years. The coaches used were already redundant from main line service but in good enough condition to convert for a further period of use as a holiday home at a time before the package tour abroad was available and affordable to the mass of people. W9928W is shown at Wargrave in the summer of 1957 with what are likely to be a posed group of holidaymakers.

British Railways

Externally perhaps covered in grime but internally still in good mechanical condition, No. 7005 *Sir Edward Elgar* rushes through Twyford from the east on its way back towards its home depôt of Worcester with the down 'Cathedrals Express' in June 1963.

Collection of Brian Davis

With the number of express and other passenger workings on the main line it is easy to forget the more humble goods workings that were just as much a part of the contemporary railway scene. To redress this imbalance the next few views show a number of the freight workings, the first a much travel-stained R.O.D. 2-8-0 No. 3043 at Waltham Sidings on 29.5.49. Unusually the train is working on the up main line. BR inherited 32 of these machines at nationalisation, the survivors of a larger class purchased second hand from the government at the end of the First World War. Few enginemen ever had a kind word for an R.O.D., they would not steam, they were uncomfortable to work and ride on, plodding on remorselessly on at their own set pace, despite all efforts of the crew.

Roger Sherlock

Another 'Bulldog' in its last days, this time No. 3418 *Sir Arthur Yorke* in the down refuge loop at Ruscombe in March 1948. Years earlier these engines had worked express passenger services on the hilly routes of Cornwall, after which it was a downward progression to pilot, secondary and branch turns and then finally goods work.

Roger Sherlock

Forerunners of the 'Bulldog' class were the smaller 'Dukes' a few of which survived into 1948 and so ended their days on freight workings. This one is renumbered No. 9076 and is of 1897 vintage, at Waltham Sidings with the all too common layers of pervading grime. The engine was finally withdrawn for scrap in 1949.

Roger Sherlock

Largest of the tank engines on the 'Western were the 54 members of the 72xx class which spent nearly all their lives on long haul freight working. Indeed I don't think I have ever seen a photograph of one on a passenger train. GWR liveried No. 7254 is shown passing Waltham in July 1948 on a long unfitted working probably bound for Acton, perhaps originating in South Wales. There were a number of these trains daily, with several devoted almost entirely to coal intended for both the industrial and domestic markets. In the foreground the down main line is laid with the new flat bottom rail whilst the remaining three running lines retain the conventional bull-head variety.

Roger Sherlock

On 25.4.54 the R.C.T.S. organised a special from Victoria to Swindon via Ealing with a pair of 'Dukedogs', Nos. 9023 and 9011, as motive power on the outward journey. The pair are seen on the down relief line between Maidenhead and Twyford running well at the head of an eight coach load. A view of the train on the return working at Goring but with a different locomotive is shown later.

W. Gilburt

As mentioned earlier through workings between Paddington and Henley-on-Thames ran during the morning and evening peaks. One of these trains is seen at Ruscombe in September 1948 and is made up of five coaches with No. 5956 *Horsley Hall* in charge. On the left the black hut is a fogmans cabin which was occupied whenever visibility was poor. The fogman was responsible for placing a detonator on the rails by the distant signal, if this was in the 'on' position, so assisting the driver by letting him know the position of the signal itself. The introduction of colour light signalling meant the end of this thankless task.

Roger Sherlock

Maidenhead was also the junction for the branches to Marlow, Bourne End and High Wycombe, most of which are out of the area covered in this volume. A Reading allocated 'Hall' No. 6923 *Croxteth Hall* at the head of a London bound train of mineral wagons passing the branch junction on a cold February day in 1963.

Tony Bennett

The appearance of a BR Standard Class '4' with a main line passenger working on the 'Western was certainly unusual. The number of WR 'Halls', 'Granges' and the like were usually sufficient to cover all available turns. No. 75002 on the down fast line at Maidenhead on 29.7.58.

Tony Molyneaux

Transition from steam and a North British built 'Warship' diesel on the up 'Mayflower' express near Maidenhead in July 1963. By this time steam had already been officially relegated from front line duties, but such was the unreliable nature of the early diesels that a train could alternate between steam and diesel haulage on consecutive days. When delays did occur the announcement of, '. . . owing to the failure of the diesel locomotive. . . .' did little to instill public confidence in the new mode of traction and so, perhaps wisely, the pronouncement was changed to '. . . locomotive failure. . . .' without reference to either steam or diesel type.

'R.A.' Collection

Furze Platt Halt was almost due north from Maidenhead on the line to Bourne End. It opened in July 1937 to serve the local community and was similar to a number of this type scattered around the GWR system and intended to meet the competition afforded by the road lobby. Most were cheaply built with only the most basic of passenger facilities.

Lens of Sutton

Part 2: South East from Reading

When referring to Reading it is easy to forget the importance of the Southern lines to the station, especially those from the south east direction and Redhill. There was also an alternative service to London (Waterloo) from Reading Southern via Bracknell, Staines and Richmond, this being operated by electric units from as far back as the mid-1930's, although it could hardly hope to compete with the Western line on either the standard of accommodation or speed. This applied even when the 'Western was totally steam operated. Certain of the passenger workings from Reading Southern, and notably the Guildford line trains remained steam hauled to the end, one of the latter shown here alongside a 2-BIL electric set in 1965.

Lens of Sutton

Contrast in electric units at Reading, that nearest the camera 4-COR set No. 3134 and alongside 4-RES No. 3072. The more usual Waterloo–Reading electric set, a 2-BIL is further on. The 'COR' and 'RES' sets worked to Reading during one week of the year only, being used on the Ascot week race trains. Both these types of units had the nickname of 'Nelsons' due to the route numbers being in the space where the secondman's window would usually be positioned. In both types of set the driver was provided with a hammock type seat which swayed with the rolling motion for which these units were renowned. On dismounting it was not unusual to see a driver similarly swaying on his feet, often to the accompaniment of ribald comments from staff and public alike.

Collection of J. Fairman

Southern Region E1 4-4-0, No. 31506 reverses out of the platform at Reading Southern towards the running shed after working a train from Redhill. The proximity of the 'Western main line can be gauged by the rear of Reading East Main signalbox in the left background. Plans for a joint station between the two companies at Reading had existed for many years, but it was left to BR to implement this on the closure of the Southern station in September 1965 when they concentrated resources at a pair of new platforms to the east end of Reading General. Alongside the running lines is the electrified, 'live', or 'juice' rail as it is called, which was partly shielded by wooden boards in the station and other areas where people might be near the track.

Tony Bennett

To service the requirements of the steam workings on the Southern side was a three road engine shed which, besides dealing with locomotives from the Redhill line, would also turn and service engines from the Southampton workings. As would be expected, the allocation also included a number of machines for freight turns although the 'Q1' depicted here did in fact originate from Feltham. Left to right then are 'N' class No. 31412, 'Q1' No. 33001 and BR Class 4 tank, No. 80085. 11.4.64.

Collection of Brian Davis

The last 'Schools' class 4-4-0's of the Southern were withdrawn in 1962 with most redundant rather than worn out. Already displaced by the electrification of the lines into Kent, a number worked the local services into Reading which was a far cry from their previous express duties. Taking water at the Southern shed is No. 30906 *Sherborne*, the sharp inclination to both the cab windows and tender sides to conform to the reduced Hastings line loading gauge.

Courtney Haydon

A pair of veterans in the Southern shed yard dwarfed by the bulk of Reading East Main signalbox behind. Both are members of the 'T' class, introduced back in 1879 and almost at the end of their days. In front is No. 1602, still with its original SR number whilst behind is No. 31604. 3.6.50.

W. Gilburt

Slighty newer than the previous design were the 'G6' 0-6-0 tanks of 1894, on which many a young fireman learnt the art of shunting with a handbrake, as this was almost the only means of stopping the engine! No. 30277 is stood in the dead end siding at the base of 'East Main complete with the early BR 'Cycling lion' emblem. It was said that one million bricks were used in the construction of the signalbox, although it is not possible to verify such a statement as the structure has been demolished for some years.

Collection of Brian Davis

An unusual visitor to Reading in the form of No. 30453 *King Arthur* and judging from its spruced up appearance it was perhaps on a special working.

Collection of Brian Davis

There was a marked family similarity between a number of Southern engines and in particular those with smoke deflectors of the style shown here. This is 'S15' 4-6-0 No. 30839, the last active member of the class, outside a deserted Reading South steam shed in May 1965 and destined eventually for Waterloo to work a special the next day.

J. Fairman

Alongside a multitude of assorted trackside fittings, 'U' class 2-6-0 No. 31809 stands on the wartime connection between the Western and Southern at Reading in March 1965. In the background the progress of modernisation is all too apparent, the semaphore signal posts being minus any arms and the replacement colour light post alongside. On the Southern line though mechanical signalling still reigned supreme. Notice too the water crane devoid of its bag and as such of no use to a steam engine. The connection in the foreground and protected by the ground disc is the low level siding from Reading Gas Works.

J. Fairman

Sunday 3.3.63 and a special working into the high level siding at Reading Gas Works. Class '5' No. 73085 is slowly propelling its train, which included a new gas cooler and the Nine Elms steam crane. The crane was for unloading the gas cooler at the required site. Unfortunately no one seemed to have been aware that such a large engine was prohibited from the siding, the flanges squealing in protest at the sharp curve. Also when the time came to unload the equipment the outriggers of the crane sank slightly into the ground on either side of the track. 'What happens if the crane starts to topple . . .?' asked a concerned gas board official. 'Oh, we'll just let it go . . .', replied a railway employee, oblivious to the fact that beneath the surface, gas and high pressure steam pipes ran parallel with the rails. Fortunately the task was completed without further incident.

Collection of J. Fairman

Further problems at Reading Gas Works, this time when an over enthusiastic shunt caused D3831 to collide with an overhead archway which promptly collapsed on to the top of the proceeding engine. This was the scene shortly after the incident with engine and brickwork both somewhat bruised. D3831 was later pulled clear by another diesel shunter with a line of open wagons as a barrier between the two. 21.9.66.

J. Fairman

For many years Reading was renowned for the famed Huntley & Palmer biscuit factory, the smell of biscuit baking a delightful aroma recalled with affection. The company had their own private siding facilities and in addition a network of sidings within the works which were shunted by two fireless locomotives. These engines were in effect steam reservoirs on wheels, carrying a charge of steam sufficient for 3–4 hours work. The use of this type of engine reduced the fire risk of working in potential danger areas, such as the packing department. The machine is just emerging from the short tunnel which connected the factories on either side of the main line. 27.5.64.

J. Fairman

Another special working and an unusual view of the privately preserved LNER Pacific *Flying Scotsman* on the Southern line at Earley. The engine is waiting for the signal to clear before continuing towards Reading and, somewhat unusually, for a special train, the whole scene is almost totally devoid of observers. 18.9.65.

J. Fairman

There were two stations at Windsor, one approached from the 'Western line at Slough and the other the Southern station on the route from Staines. Both are still open today but with no physical connection between the two. On 30.4.66 the Southern station was host to a rail tour which originated at Waterloo and took in the Longmoor Military Railway before visiting Windsor. A variety of motive power was used, although for the first and last legs 'U' class 2-6-0's Nos. 31791 and 31639 were in charge, the pair seen departing against the background of the Royal Castle.

J. Fairman

An earlier tour to Windsor was with an Adams radial tank No. 30582 on 19.3.61. Engines of this type had worked the steam suburban services to the town sixty years earlier, but were displaced from such duties by electrification. Three of the type survived, and for many years were in sole charge of traffic on the Lyme Regis branch although this came to an end in 1961. No. 30582 working a roundabout route to Eastleigh from Lyme Regis and eventual withdrawal.

Tony Bennett

Part 3: The Basingstoke Branch from Reading

Running south and west from Reading was the former Berks and Hants Company line to Basingstoke and Devizes. The GWR had absorbed the route into its own organisation back in the 19th century yet, in steam days and even today the route west is still known as the Berks & Hants. Besides the West of England express services that used the B & H there were a number of stopping services to both Basingstoke and Hungerford, most of which started from the bays at the west end of Reading station, indeed just as the counterpart diesel services still do today. This is probably a Basingstoke working with 61xx No. 6145 at its head at what is now Platform 3. The diesel railcar alongside has just arrived on a stopping service from Newbury. 12.5.51.

Philip Kelley

Sunday relaying work by the Berks and Hants junction, with something like 34 men visible most of whom appear to be supervising! The crane lifting the rails was one of a number allocated to the Reading civil engineers department whose area, besides covering the station itself, included the B & H lines to Basingstoke & Hungerford, the Lambourn & D.N. & S. routes, the main line to Didcot and Twyford and the Wallingford and Henley branches.

'R. A.' Collection

The signalman's view of No. 5944 *Ickenham Hall* as it takes the B & H route by Reading West Main 'box on a stopping train to Newbury. This was an afternoon working made up of Southern Region stock from an earlier Basingstoke arrival. In the left background is a glimpse of the Western steam shed which is referred to in several pictures further on. No. 5944's tender is loaded with what appears to be mainly slack, no doubt much to the annoyance of the fireman.

Collection of Brian Davis

54

Reading West was the third station serving the town and was situated on the B & H line less than one mile from Reading General. Trains approaching from the south could either take the route east towards London or use what was known as the east curve to run west towards Didcot. Both routes are still open today with the actual point of divergence, known as Oxford Road junction, visible beyond the platform canopy. Despite its small size compared with its neighbours, Reading West boasted a station master for many years, one of the best remembered being Ted Carpenter who had several relations who were also railway employees. In this quite delightful view No. 7924 *Thornycroft Hall* runs through the station bound for the West Country with a train from Paddington comprising of Hawksworth stock. Notice also the 'Brylcreem' advert on the end of the station building . . . !

Collection of P.T. Earl

Leaving a smoke screen across the afternoon sky, No. 34029 *Lundy* makes a spirited get away from Reading West with the southbound 'Pines Express' on 3.5.63. As a prelude to the closure of the Somerset & Dorset line this train was diverted to run from Poole via Southampton, Basingstoke, Reading and Oxford with a Bournemouth engine and crew instead of Branksome men – hence the duty number 399 on the headcode disc. To avoid a reversal at Reading General the train took the east curve although in doing so any passengers for Reading itself would either find themselves forced to change and await a connection via a local train or walk. Today the inter-regional trains still run via Reading but do indeed reverse at the main station, often leading to worried comments from passengers not aware of this method of operating.

Collection of Brian Davis

Back to a more conventional train, a Southern 'King Arthur' No. 30789 *Sir Guy* on a freight probably bound for Salisbury via Basingstoke. After a number of years on passenger workings the class spent their last years on a mixture of goods and other workings. Withdrawals commenced in the late 1950's and with No. 30789 an early casualty.

Collection of Roger Simmonds

Besides the locomotive exchange trials of 1948, Swindon continued a programme of on-road locomotive testing and performance assessment right up to its demise as a main rail workshop. A number of these tests included monitoring the output of the new BR 'Standard' engines including the solitary Class 8 Pacific, No. 71000 *Duke of Gloucester*. The engine is seen just south of Reading West on a working from Swindon complete with dynamometer car. At the front of the engine in place of the smoke deflectors is a wooden indicator shelter where perhaps two men from the test staff would assist in gauging the performance. Not the ideal place to be with the engine working hard.

M.W. Earley

A Western Region freight this time, with Reading based 22xx No. 3219 at the head of an up train of tank cars near Southcote Junction, possibly from the Ministry of Supply sidings at Padworth near Aldermaston. Notice the two open wagons between the tender and tank cars which were intended to act as a barrier separating the locomotive from the inflammable cargo. A similar arrangement existed at the rear of the train ahead of the brake van and was intended to provide a barrier in the event of a bank engine or shunt taking place. Notice also the standard WR bracket signal which replaced the earlier wooden variant depicted in the next view. Left to right the signal arms refer to, Reading Central Goods, the Basingstoke branch and B & H line towards Newbury.

Collection of P.T. Earl

Wrong line working on a Sunday in 1951. 'King' class No. 6012 *King Edward VI* in the short-lived BR blue livery in charge of the down 'Cornish Riviera Express' which had been brought to a stand at Southcote Junction due to engineering work. This also involved single line running on the former up line and so the signals have not been pulled off due to the train being on the wrong line. To the right is the branch leading off to Coley, or Reading Central Goods to give the correct title. The smoke and steam was evidently arranged with the crew beforehand and a number of enquiring heads can be seen leaning from the windows of the train.

M. W. Earley

Southern Region M7 tank, No. 30108 in Coley Yard on the 'Rambling Rose' special of 23.3.63. This was a Bournemouth based engine and so was some few miles from its home depôt.

Tony Bennett

Another 'King Arthur', this time No. 30788 *Sir Urre of the Mount*, working hard on the climb near Mortimer with a SR bound freight. As referred to earlier the line south from Reading to Basingstoke was originally under 'Western control but from 2.4.50 the Southern took over from Southcote Junction. It remains under SR autonomy today.

Collection of P.T. Earl

Passing Mortimer station in late July 1965 on a through north–south working is No. 73117, the generally shabby appearance of the engine was unfortunately typical of steam by this time. This engine was originally named *Vivien* although the nameplate had been removed to prevent theft. Twenty Standard 5's allocated to the Southern were given the names of withdrawn 'King Arthur' class engines. The station building at Mortimer dates from the earliest days of the B & H line and is to Brunel's chalet style with overhanging canopy. It still survives today, probably the last brick building of its type, although ironically no longer under WR control. The origins of the station in the days of the broad gauge are also apparent and with the gap between the up and down lines much wider than usual.

R. A. Lissenden

Near the Berkshire–Hampshire border, 2-6-2 tank No. 6145 is at the head of a Basingstoke train. On either side of the running lines the permanent way department have tidied the edge of the ballast so that it neatly parallels the rails. At one time a plank was laid on its edge to assist in producing this effect. In addition the access alongside is maintained as suitable for cycling over, most important when a sudden call out for fogmans duties involved a bicycle ride to the appropriate distant signal.

Collection of P.T. Earl

Finally on the Basingstoke branch a Southern engine on a Reading working with S11 class 4-4-0 No. 30397. BR had inherited a number of engines from the Southern with this wheel arrangement, most of which were only suitable for light duties similar to that shown here. The S11 class in particular would roll at speed, partly due to the high pitch of the boiler, all were scrapped by 1960.

Collection of P.T. Earl

Part 4: The B & H Line to Newbury

Taking the West of England line at Southcote Junction is one of the later series Castle's. The Basingstoke branch diverges to the right.

Collection of Brian Davis

Detail for the modeller in this rear view of Theale signalbox in 1965. The telegraph pole alongside is an obvious feature, but not perhaps the cables running down and then across the back of the 'box before entering via a hole in the back wall. Note also the rain water butt and battery cabinets.

Philip Kelley

Just beyond Theale were a number of sidings used by the CCE department as a pre-assembly depôt. Here sections of track as well as more complex items of pointwork were made up ready for installation at the required site. In this way is was possible to iron out potential problems rather than perhaps be faced with difficulties later. During spring 1955, No. 5993 *Kirby Hall* was in charge of a demonstration train for testing ways of unloading rail, although as one piece has landed on its side this may well have been a none too successful test.

British Railways

The 'Grange' class 4-6-0's were equipped with smaller wheels than the Hall's and were consequently ideal for slightly lighter trains. Four coaches though was a featherweight load for No. 6860 *Aberporth Grange*, depicted near Aldermaston on a local passenger service.

Hugh Davies

Another useful detail view and this time of Aldermaston goods shed. Notice the loading gauge built into the siding opening, with the gauge itself slightly offset, which may well indicate that the shed once housed broad gauge track. During the Second World War the GWR had removed many of their offices from Paddington to a number of buildings near Aldermaston with a special train run each way daily for the benefit of the displaced personnel. This working ceased shortly after the return to peacetime, although for many years there was a reminder in the notice by the office which read 'Staff proceeding to the offices MUST NOT WALK ALONG THE LINE but must use the authorised route via the station approach road'.

Philip Kelley

Midgham station was originally called Woolhampton but to avoid confusion with Wolverhampton the name was changed very early on. No. 4919 *Donnington Hall* passing the station level-crossing on 5.8.61 on down milk empties. This was one of six level-crossings on the B & H line between Southcote and Hungerford.

Philip Kelley

Close-up detail of Midgham station and a variety of now long vanished items on view. Notice the drop case station clock, the GWR fire buckets and 1*d*. Nestle's chocolate machine. A quick kick at the base of the latter together with a grab for the handle was often sufficient to produce a bar without payment . . . !

Collection of P.T. Earl

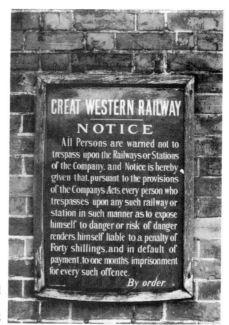

Another almost forgotten relic which once adorned almost every station.

Tony Molyneaux

Just west of Thatcham station and alongside the main line an Ordnance Depôt was established around 1940. This was worked by a number of steam engines, with in later years the standard Austerity 0-6-0 tanks as the most common. The army locomotives were used for shunting within the site as well as forming trains at the nearby interchange sidings with BR.

David Abbott

One of the prestigious race specials at Newbury Racecourse behind No. 6000 *King George V*. The practice of running special trains in conjunction with the race meetings is one which has continued up to the present day, although in a somewhat abridged form. During the days of steam so great was the importance placed upon these workings, especially the members only train which ran non-stop from Paddington, that an Inspector would be provided to oversee operations at the station for the day. After arrival engines were turned on the turntable specially provided and were so ready for the return working later in the afternoon.

Collection of J. Fairman

No. 6994 *Baggrave Hall* ready to depart from the up main platform with a fast passenger working from Weymouth in August 1956. During the days prior to nationalisation the GWR and SR had competed over the Weymouth traffic, each running trains over their own lines as far as the junction at Dorchester, just short of the final destination. GWR and later WR trains took the route from Paddington to Reading and thence via Newbury, Westbury, Castle Cary and Yeovil. Between Paddington and Newbury there was just one booked stop at Reading, so providing Newbury with a fast service to the capital. Unfortunately, the operation of what was in reality a duplicate service eventually came to the notice of BR and, although Newbury still retains its services to Paddington and the West Country the direct Weymouth services were taken off some years ago. Behind the engine is another bay platform used by stopping services to Reading and Didcot.

W. Gilburt

Newbury, down side, depicted in 1967 and although the buildings are perhaps little altered, a number of the types of car shown have all but vanished. Beyond the footbridge and station buildings was a bay platform together with two other sidings, one of these used as a loading dock. The bay was referred to as the 'Winchester Bay' as it was from here that many of the trains to Winchester and Southampton would depart. Its use for stopping services to Hungerford and Westbury was seemingly overlooked. On the loading bank opposite was a grounded coach body, originally the local railway Temperance Institute and Great Western coffee tavern, it is perhaps best remembered in its later role as a shoe repairers. Nearer the camera the plain brick building with a flat roof was originally an air raid shelter.

'R.A.' Collection

Busy times on the London bound side at Newbury with the arrival of the 8.30 a.m. Plymouth–
Paddington express just after midday on 13.7.67. At the head is a maroon liveried 'Western' diesel,
which along with the smaller 'Hymeks' were thought by many to be amongst the best looking
diesel locomotives ever produced – no wonder, a number were built at Swindon. . . !

'R.A.' Collection

Part 5: The D.N. & S. Line

At Newbury there were connections with the north–south lines to Didcot and Winchester as well as the little branch to Lambourn. All three routes are now just a memory. Heading south for Newbury near Churn and past the open space of the Berkshire Downs, 57xx series pannier tank No. 4649 is at the head of a three coach train from Didcot. Just to the left of the engine and partly hidden from view by the exhaust is a board 'Prize Length' and an indication that the track gang responsible for the section had recently won a railway competition for the condition of their piece of track.

J.F. Russell Smith/National Railway Museum

Churn station is particularly remembered by some as the location where many a conscript spent his first nights under canvas during the days of National service. Aside from this it can also lay claim to being one of the few railway stopping places without any form of road access and consequently patronage was poor. Indeed intending passengers were requested to give a hand signal to the driver as the train approached. Today its windswept and desolate platform probably sees more visitors than ever before as it has become a popular place for walkers and hikers, a place to sit and ponder over a railway that is no more.

Lens of Sutton

High among the windswept downlands of rural Berkshire, *City of Truro* heads north for Didcot with a stopping service from Southampton.

Hugh Davies

72

'T9' No. 30117 at Compton, D.N. & S. line.

Lens of Sutton

A re-arrangement of regional boundaries meant the D.N. & S. line south of Newbury was transferred to Southern Region control from April 1950. At first this had little effect upon the workings over the line, but some time later Eastleigh men were faced with the prospect of working trains to Newbury and Didcot whilst the Didcot crews could find they would take over a strange Southern machine for part of their duty.

One of the first times this occurred was at Newbury, when a pair of Eastleigh men arrived at the head of a 'T9' from Southampton and after shunting to the up-bay platform handed over the engine to a Didcot crew who would complete the journey. This was the first time the 'Western men had been on a 'T9' and several unfavourable comments were passed as to the prospects of working such '. . . ancient Southern old iron . . .' compared with their usual 22xx engines.

After a series of trial and error moves aimed at discovering what, where and how the various controls operated the fireman had learnt that the water feed to the injectors was activated by kicking a pedal on the floor. This alone was totally alien, but unknown to them, the standard fitting on a lot of South Western engines.

Western engine men always tried to run to with a full glass of water in the boiler, and the old 'T9' which is displaying only half a glass is paramount to dropping a fusible plug. 'Better get some more in the boiler mate . . .', remarks the driver and so the fireman manipulates, kicks and generally curses the various controls until with a gurgle resembling a fish fryer the injector picks to fill the boiler with water.

Later it was said the 'Western men had been warned not to attempt to run a 'T9' with more than half a glass, but old habits die hard and soon the water was out of sight in the gauge glass. Now when this happened, and before there was any change of note from the injector, the front end was full of chalky white water and it was only then that the injector started to cough and it was rapidly turned off.

Outside the three coach train was rapidly starting to fill. School-children going home from Newbury to Compton and others after a day at the market. Being a warm day the windows were open and doors kept ajar until such time as the train was ready to depart. In addition quietly strolling along the platform was an immaculate guard, his trousers pressed with a knife edge crease and a carnation in the button hole of his uniform jacket. To the railway this may well have

73

been a branch line service, but to the guard this was no reason for allowing the standards of yesteryear to slip.

At that moment the signal at the end of the platform fell to the 'off' position. The guard anxious to be away consulted his watch and started back to his van blowing his whistle in the process.

As if in response to this a light breeze began to blow backwards from the engine whilst a number of heads emerged from the carriage windows to observe the departure. The guard blew his whistle again and waved his flag, the driver tried to blow the engine whistle but instead there was a strangled rasp. He then tried to release the brakes and only succeeded after much gurgling from the vacuum exhaust pipe in the chimney. Still neither driver or fireman realised their error.

Then came the fatal mistake, the driver moved the steam reverser into full forward gear and opened the throttle just as he would on a 22xx . . . It was a wonder the coupling rods didn't break, the 'T9' heaved, shook and tried her very best to move forward but that white pickle had penetrated every steam passage there was and instead of forward travel the only movement came from a white froth that emerged from the chimney and was blown back along the train.

All this takes much longer to write than it took to happen and as the breeze blew so blonde, ginger and dark hair became snow white, the young ladies with their summer dresses took on a speckled pattern and the guard's previously highly polished shoes began to look like cricket boots.

As for the engine itself it was covered from end to end in a white sludge, whilst to cap it all the 'T9' by now back to just half a glass of water began to blow off steam violently from the safety valve and of course this dislodged even more sludge to deposit itself lovingly around passengers and staff alike.

A mass of bodies dislodged themselves from the train and rapidly made their way to the station toilets where an apologetic staff tried their level best to effect calm. Departure was eventually 20 minutes late and it didn't help the crew later when recounting the story to a former Southern man who was heard to remark, 'They be nice little engines my dear, but 'e mustn't fill 'em up. . . .'

Hugh Abbinnett

74

Hampstead Norris station on the line from Didcot to Newbury and with Collett design 22xx, No. 2252 at the head of a Southampton train. These engines were regular performers on the D.N. & S. line, well suited to the terrain and not too heavy loads. Schedules too were easy, with something like 45 minutes allowed for the 18 miles inclusive of six intermediate stops.

E.T. Gill

A classic study of the daily pick up freight once so typical of the railway scene. Unfortunately it is also apparent how hopelessly uneconomic such services were, as 22xx No. 2289 wends it leisurely way along the D.N. & S. line not far from Hampstead Norris.

J.F. Russell Smith / National Railway Museum

At Newbury the line from Didcot joined the main Berks and Hants route east of the station necessitating slowing down to 10 mph for the junction, although this was not always strictly adhered too. This 1957 view taken from the first coach shows the train as it joins the down main line and about to pass the goods yard on the short distance to Newbury station.

R.M. Casserley

A grey February day in 1960 finds 2-8-0 No. 2841 heading west through Newbury on a permanent way train. This was a sad year for railways locally, as in January the Lambourn line had closed to passengers whilst just a little later in March the same fate befell the direct service to Winchester.

P.J. Cupper

The story of how the famous 4-4-0 *City of Truro* was resurrected for service in 1957 already well known, the bright livery a welcome attraction against the generally sombre appearance of the rural D.N. & S. line. Here the engine is just west of Newbury on its way to Enborne Junction and the line south, the rail on the extreme left is part of the Lambourn branch.

R.M. Casserley

South of Newbury the first station towards Winchester was at Woodhay, pronounced 'Woody' by the local porter. It was also the end of the double track section from Enborne. No. 5381 about to shut off steam ready for the station stop with a Southampton bound passenger train in April 1951.

J.F. Russell Smith/National Railway Museum

Although just over the border into Hampshire I could not resist including this superb view of No. 3212 on a Newbury train just south of Woodhay. Today the stretch of line south of the station is desolate and overgrown, yet there is talk of using it for part of the Newbury relief road at some time in the future. Before the railway arrived on the scene in 1885 a cart-way had run over the same course, the wheel has indeed turned its full circle.

J.F. Russell Smith/National Railway Museum

Part 6: The Lambourn Branch

Back at Newbury, trains for the Lambourn branch used their own separate bay at the west end of the up platform. This was equipped with an engine release crossover so that the branch loco could run round without needing to occupy the main line – although it did depend on the loop itself being free of obstructions. On this occasion the loop would appear to have been occupied and so the 57xx pannier tank would have to find some other means of attaching itself to the opposite end of its coach before the return trip up the valley to the terminus.

R. Denison

Trains on the Lambourn branch were operated by a mixture of either steam or diesel, this branch being one of the first to be worked by railcar as far back as 1936. Ironically the diesels themselves were later replaced by steam again during the last years. In the early part of 1948 both forms of transport can be seen, with the effects of the horrendous weather of that time still visible.

E. Best

With no turntable at Lambourn, tender engines were faced with the prospect of running in reverse for half the journey, with the crews deciding which way this would be according to the prevailing weather conditions. (The relaxed schedules allowed for use of the turntable at the Racecourse station.) During 1950 a 'Dean Goods' was in charge of the branch service while in the background a railcar occupies the bay platform. This indicates that the steam train was the 4.15 p.m. service, known locally as the school train, which returned empty from Lambourn at 5.08 p.m.

P.J. Garland

The daily freight for Lambourn about to join the branch at Newbury and with former MSWJ 2-4-0 No. 1336 in charge. As the train is made up of only seven vehicles the driver may well be content to take things easy, for had a longer train been involved, it was the practice to take a run at the branch from almost the whole length of the up platform. This being the only way to ensure the load would successfully surmount the climb towards West Fields and Speen.

N. E. Stead

There were three level-crossings on the branch with the first at Speen, only a short distance out of Newbury. All the gates at these crossings were hand operated for which the station porter was responsible during his hours of duty. Even so it was not unknown for a train to arrive at Lambourn with the front festooned with bits of matchwood, perhaps where the porter was occupied with other tasks and the driver had not been as alert as he might. A single coach diesel railcar depicted as the branch service at Speen during the early 1950's.

B.Y. Williams

Like so many other rural railways the Lambourn branch blended in well with the landscape although again on economic grounds it is a wonder it lasted as long as it did. For the locomotive crews a trip on the branch was regarded as a day out, away from the hustle and bustle of the main line, with time to stop and chat, perhaps even to gather mushrooms to fry on the shovel. In this view time has surely stood still, the fireman posed on the running plate with just a wisp of steam from the injector overflow. Notice too the hay rick in the background, No. 1336 on its way up the valley with a single wagon of coal for the local merchant.

J.F. Russell Smith/National Railway Museum

The use of diesel railcars on the branch had advantages as well as drawbacks, for whilst there was a saving in that no fireman was needed, the units were incapable of drawing unfitted wagons so a single load of coal, as shown in the previous view, meant the use of a special steam working. During peak hours too the passenger accommodation could also be cramped although on this occasion at Welford Park the signalman is one of the few people present.

B.Y. Williams

Welford Park was approximately mid-way along the branch and the only place where a loop was provided to cross trains. Accordingly a diminutive signalbox also existed with the signalman responsible for issuing tickets and dealing with the general porters duties in addition to his normal role. Even so his duties were hardly strenuous as Welford Park was amongst the quietest of all the branch stations. As ever though there is an exception, such as in 1951 when an enthusiasts special arrived. The various enthusiasts were seen to swarm everywhere with one wag holding up the balance weights so that both signals showed 'off'.

'R.A.' Collection

Welford Park, a more respectable goods train this time with No. 1335 another of the MSWJ 2-4-0's at its head. The three engines of this type which survived into nationalised ownership were allocated around the Oxford, Didcot and Reading areas and were ideally suited for this type of light branch duty.

Collection of P. T. Earl

1959 was the last year of passenger operation on the branch, 22xx No. 2214 about to leave Welford Park for Lambourn with a two coach load during what is remembered as a gloriously long summer. As would perhaps be expected passenger accommodation at the station was spartan and consisted of a single corrugated shelter on each platform. Until the building of the military sidings the signalbox backed directly onto a field which for a while was occupied by a number of horses. One of these animals had the annoying habit of gnawing at the rear timbers of the 'box causing considerable fright to the signalman the first time it occurred.

D.W. Winkworth

Aside from its notoriety as the location of one of the stately homes of Berkshire, Welford Park was also the name given to an air base established during the war years from which a number of secret glider experiments took place. During the early 1950's a change of role was decided upon for the base and it was converted instead to the storage of munitions. Rail access was also decided upon and a new branch line built from the Lambourn branch to the base, two sets of interchange sidings were also provided. Shown here is a stage in the construction of the new sidings at Welford with the original railway on the extreme right. The contractors used a number of light steam engines in the course of the work, one of the last times this took place at any civil engineering location in the country.

British Railways

The next station along from Welford Park was Great Shefford and once again in charge of a single porter. Here at least passengers were afforded the luxury of a timber waiting shelter with a notice pinned to the door stating that, 'ALL TICKETS MUST BE SHEWN'. Awaiting the 'right-away' is a 57xx series pannier tank on a train for Lambourn.

R. Denison

Contrasting shades of wet and dry at Lambourn with No. 4665 after arrival at the terminus with the single coach service from Newbury on 10.10.59. The train can be seen to have stopped short of the protection afforded by the station canopy and necessarily so as the engine had to allow sufficient room to run round clear of its coach. Above the smokebox there is a chalked inscription 'Romeo'.

R.A. Lissenden

Tender first back to Newbury and a Collett 22xx leaves Lambourn on the return run down the valley. Despite passenger loadings being small, receipts were augmented by the conveyance of race-horses from what is still the foremost training area in the county. Although as time passed more and more of this traffic was switched to road vehicles. Two rail horseboxes can be seen in the background whilst perhaps the greatest irony of all is that the station area is nowadays the headquarters of one of the road horsebox operators.

G. Siviour

Part 7: The B & H West of Newbury

A final visit to Newbury with a scene so well recalled even for the main line. Later series 57xx pannier tank No. 8720 rattles through the station towards Reading on the pick up goods with just one box van and a brake.

E. Best

West of Newbury now towards Kintbury with the railway almost parallel with the earlier Kennet and Avon Canal – although the canal is not visible in this particular view. No. 2950 *Taplow Court* is on the down 2.35 p.m. Paddington–West of England express passing Enborne Junction, 21.7.51.

J.F. Russell Smith/National Railway Museum

The big 47xx 2-8-0's were rarely seen on daytime duties and instead spent most of their time on heavy fitted trains most of which were run at night. But in the summer peaks it was a different matter and right through the 1950's these superbly proportioned machines could be seen on relief duties at a time when the same train would perhaps need to be run in three or even four parts, so great were the number of passengers. Such was the case in the summer of 1952, with a rather grimy No. 4703 working hard near Hungerford at the head of the second part of the 1.25. p.m. Paddington–Plymouth, made up of 11 coaches perhaps weighing 400 tons including its compliment of passengers. None of the nine engines in the class survived to be preserved.

Collection of P. T. Earl

By the 1950's there were few members of the 'Star' class remaining in first rate condition, their former top link duties had been taken over by the later design Castle's and King's. As a reminder then of days almost past, No. 4020 *Knight Commander* puts up a smokescreen near Bedwyn on the 1.40 p.m. Paddington–Penzance train on 29.7.50, which the engine will probably haul as far as Plymouth.

Collection of P. T. Earl

Part 8: The Western Shed at Reading

Returning again to Reading and this time to the 'Western engine shed which was in a dip within the triangle formed by the main line and curves of the Berks & Hants. In steam days the shed was one of the major depôts in the London division with an allocation of around 100 engines, although, not all of course would be present at the same time. Today the diesel depôt occupies the same site whilst the stabling point for the modern D.M.U's was formally the carriage sidings. SR 'D1' 4-4-0 passing the shed after arrival light from Basingstoke.

Collection of Brian Davis

A sad sight for the steam enthusiast with No. 6871, formally *Bourton Grange* leaving the shed with a collection of withdrawn engines destined for the scrapyard.

Collection of J. Fairman

The shed itself had nine roads four of which ran through. Besides a number of other sidings there were also two lines around the southern perimeter, *Mogul* No. 6337, seen on one of these bound for the shed exit next to Reading West Junction.

Collection of Brian Davis

Refilling with water, whether on a tank or tender engine, was a team effort. One man to steady the heavy leather bag and the other to operate the control valve as needed. Caution was also needed as should the water level rise too fast the bag would jump free drenching anyone in its path. In winter especially this was a none too pleasant prospect, many a crew attempting to dry out their overalls in front of the firebox and hopefully hiding their modesty from view.

Collection of Brian Davis

An unfortunate occurrance happened at Reading during the 1950's when a cleaner fell from a wooden trestle while working. Legal action against the railway followed and in connection with this a series of photographs were taken to help illustrate the incident. The pannier tank alongside was temporarily whitewashed to assist in the quality of the photograph – why it was not just moved is not clear. In practice few men would use these trestles, preferring instead to clamber along the narrow edge of the tender body holding on with one hand to the top rail.

British Railways

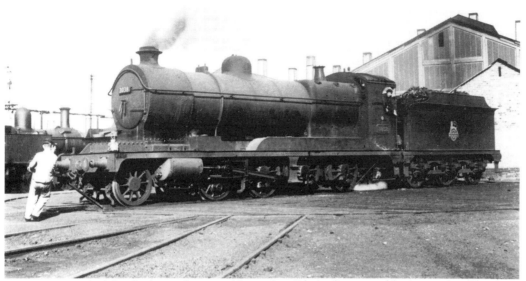

At the west end of the shed was the turntable, and at 65ft. in diameter able to cater for all engines likely to use it. Unlike a number of sites, particularly on the other regions, muscle power was needed, although this was reasonably easy provided the engine was properly balanced. R.O.D. 2-8-0 No. 3038 of Pontypool Road shed is being turned ready to head back towards South Wales on 23.4.50.

W. Gilburt

Prior to the closure of the Southern shed in 1965 it was unusual to see a former SR engine in the 'Western shed. Exceptions though could happen and usually when the facilities at Reading Southern were temporarily out of action for servicing. This may well have been the reason for the appearance of No. 30783 *Sir Gillemere* at the Western shed in June 1950 after arriving with a train from Basingstoke.

W. Gilburt

Checking the tyre pressures perhaps, or maybe kick it if it won't go? Not really, the man is probably trying to remove some grease from his overalls with waste steam from the cylinder cocks. No. 4074 *Caldicot Castle* in beautifully clean brunswick green livery outside Reading shed.

Collection of Brian Davis

A number of Hall's were allocated to Reading, one of these No. 6996 *Blackwell Hall* posed outside the shed in June 1950 with No. 4989 *Cherwell Hall* almost hidden from view behind. The engine tender is noticably devoid of any signs of ownership which was a relatively common feature in the years immediately following nationalisation.

W. Gilburt

The final development of the ubiquitous pannier tank was the 94xx class still with the standard inside 2-cylinder layout. Where other companies had gone for a side tank design, the use of panniers allowed ease of access to the inside motion for lubrication and servicing and was in practice a successful arrangement. No. 8430 was one of the class built to the Swindon design by W. Bagnell in 1953, other members of the class being introduced as late as 1956. The engine had probably just received a boiler washout as both the covers from the firebox wash out plugs are hanging down, care would also be needed to sweep off the coal from the cab roof before the engine was steamed again for service. 24.3.62.

Courtney Haydon

It was a sad fact that concurrent with the demise of the steam engine was a reduction in cleaning standards. No. 6858 *Woolston Grange* in August 1964 unfortunately typical of so many engines in later years. The engine is outside the front of Reading steam shed, the corrugated building behind is the depôt repair shop. Notice also the warning flashes for overhead live wires affixed to the boiler and firebox sides. This was then standard practice for all locomotives, regardless of the fact that the engine was never likely to stray into a 25kV. electrified area.

Roger Sherlock

The BR standard engines were not universally popular with all crews, for although they were certainly efficient and reliable performers, company loyalties died hard. Accordingly, it was in certain areas that they received the most acclaim, particularly where they replaced a number of elderly designs that really should have been consigned to the scrap heap years earlier. As far as the Western Region was concerned the men preferred their own Swindon machines, although not all that many miles away at Eastleigh the reverse was the case. No. 76005 is seen outside Reading shed and illuminated to superb effect by a low winter sun. Alongside is another feature now almost forgotten, a fire devil, intended to prevent the water column from freezing.

Collection of Brian Davis

No. 5927 *Guild Hall*, a 22xx and pannier tanks at Reading, with an obvious contrast in external condition. Compared with the relative cleanliness associated with the present Reading diesel depôt the amount of ash, coal and other debris on the ground is appalling and yet was unfortunately typical of every steam shed in the country. It was in this environment that engines were serviced, prepared for and disposed of after duty, yet the men took it to be a normal feature of their daily work. No wonder the Offices, Shops & Railway Premises Act deliberately excluded locomotive sheds, to do otherwise would have brought the system to a halt overnight!

Collection of Brian Davis

Another SR based standard, No. 76014 of Eastleigh shed at Reading. As first introduced these engines were amongst the last steam designs to be allocated to a regular crew, which paid dividends when it came to reduced maintainance requirements.

Collection of Brian Davis

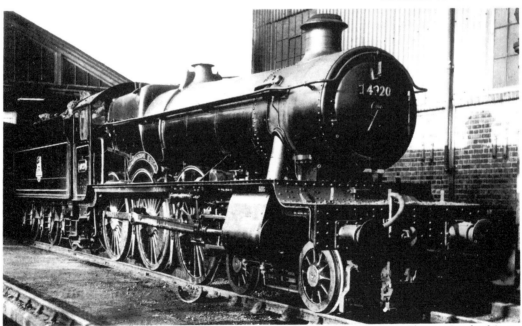

The now preserved No. 4920 *Dumbleton Hall* outside Reading shed in 1949. The engine had just been into shops for overhaul and had emerged in the original BR mixed traffic livery of lined black. A reversion to green came later. At the time the view was taken no shed plate was affixed and instead 'RDG' was painted on the footplate valance in pre-nationalisation style – why BR later went to the expense of casting allocation plates for thousands of engines is a mystery. Notice also the 'X' marking above the cab side number, meaning this engine was permitted to take loads above that normally stipulated in the working timetable.

Collection of Brian Davis

Big Prarie, No. 6130 at Reading with its front driving wheels temporarily removed to facilitate repair. Scenes like this were common in steam days yet rarely were they recorded on film.

J. Fairman

Ex-LMS 4F, No. 44334 of Rowsley shed at Reading on Good Friday, 27.3.64. The engine was awaiting repairs to a big end bearing and eventually returned north to its home shed some eight weeks later.

J. Fairman

The Austerity design 2-8-0's were introduced during the Second World War to relieve a chronic locomotive shortage, with the vast majority subsequently taken over by BR. As with the later standard classes they were not universally popular and this is perhaps exemplified by the shocking external condition. This is supposedly No. 70876 at Reading in April 1950, although some confusion may exist over the actual number. All the class were later re-numbered by BR in the 77xxx and finally 90xxx series.

W. Gilburt

Constructed back in 1883, '850' class saddle tank No. 1925 just survived into nationalisation and is seen at Reading in June 1950 ten months before withdrawal. The antiquated design is apparent in the open cab, with the only protection for the crew by means of the storm sheet at present folded on the top of the roof. Saddle tanks had generally been superseded by the pannier variant many years earlier and a number of the '850' class were so converted. In its last years, No. 1925 was used on the Lambourn branch as well as for shunting at Reading, much of this within the confines of the signal works. Notice the fire irons in the standard position for tank engines on the back of the bunker.

W. Gilburt

Temporarily resident at Reading, No. 6027 *King Richard I* inside the lifting shop and receiving attention to a hot bearing on the front bogie. As a result of its failure the engine had come off its train at the station and had to be repaired as necessary before returning to duty.

Collection of Brian Davis

Part 9: West of Reading

Time for a breather between duties and the crew of No. 6923 *Croxteth Hall* perhaps awaiting a signal to clear. The letter 'D' on the cabside is an indication of the power catagory. Hanging from the cab is the 'pep-pipe' used for damping down coal dust on the tender.

Collection of Brian Davis

A day out at the races perhaps, 'Dukedog' No. 9028 at the head of four horse-boxes and a passenger brake on the up main line at Scours Lane just west of Reading. The engine carries an '84J' shedplate and was allocated to Croes Newydd shed at Wrexham so is a long way from home. It was likely this was a train which originated from Holyhead and was destined for Lambourn with brood mares bought at the Irish bloodstock sales. Worth mentioning is the ATC ramp visible directly ahead of the engine.

Collection of Brian Davis

Another view which dates the railway scene, brand new BMC cars, including Minis, 1100's, MG Midget's, a Cambridge and the much loved Morris Minor. The train is passing Scours Lane with the covered vans also containing cars. In charge is another Eastleigh engine, No. 75065, the consignment possibly bound for export from Southampton. Do notice the wires and point rodding associated with mechanical signalling parallel with the track, the up and down main lines both laid with flat bottom rail.

Collection of Brian Davis

The Western Region heavy freight design, a later 28xx series engine, No. 3854 pulling away from Reading West yard with a Class 'H' through freight. Although undated this is probably towards the end of steam as the engine has its smokebox door hinges picked out in white, a feature of the final years.

Collection of Brian Davis

For a time during the late 1950's a few LMS design 8F's were allocated to Old Oak Common shed and used to augment the 28xx and 38xx series 2-8-0's on freight workings. Many of the 'Western men were already familiar with the type as a number had been built at Swindon during 1942. Probably the most obvious difference was in the left hand driving position, with the opposite side being used on every 'Western engine. No. 48431 is working hard on the down relief near Tilehurst with a heavy freight in August 1961.

Tony Molyneaux

Probably on a transfer working between the yards at Didcot and Reading, No. 8496 coasts through Tilehurst on the up relief line with a mixed freight including several containers. This type of traffic, it was hoped, would be the saviour of rail bourne freight, with the railway publicity department advertising a 'DOR to DOR' service which included road collection and delivery. Unfortunately amongst other problems the containers themselves proved too small for all types of traffic.

Tony Molyneaux

A feature of the last days of steam was the almost endless variety of special workings, a compliment to both the organizers of such tours as well as an enterprising railway management. Some of these trips involved the use of engines alien to the local area, such as when a former LNER 'A4', No. 60024 *Kingfisher* was booked to work a special on the Southern Region between Waterloo and Yeovil – a long way from its more usual haunts on the Glasgow to Edinburgh line. As a means of bringing the locomotive south it was used on a variety of turns, and is seen passing Tilehurst on 22.3.66 with the 11.10 a.m. Banbury to Eastleigh freight.

J. Fairman

It would not be possible to leave Tilehurst without a brief mention of the superb floral display afforded by the station gardens and a tribute to the two men here, Frank and Jack. Years earlier the railways had awarded prizes for the best kept station gardens in a particular area, with most of the awards being won by the various branch line locations. Tilehurst though was the exception and belied its position as a country station on a busy main line.

'R. A.' Collection

No. 34004, which formally carried the name *Yeovil*, shatters the tranquility of the Thames Valley at Pangbourne as it heads south with the afternoon Newcastle–Bournemouth through working. The Pacific will have taken over the train at Oxford having previously worked a similar service north earlier in the day.

J. Fairman

With the cold February air causing the exhaust to condense into white clouds, No. 6983 *Otterington Hall* heads east on the up relief line at Pangbourne in 1965.

J. Fairman

There were two sets of water troughs in Berkshire, near Aldermaston on the B & H line and on the main line just east of Goring. Both locations were a favourite with photographers as an amount of spray was produced by the effect of the engine picking up water at speed. In this view taken at Goring in the summer of 1950, No. 2837 replenishes its tender at a more sedate pace as it heads west with a long train of empty wagons.

Collection of P. T. Earl

The return working of the Victoria–Swindon–Highworth special depicted earlier. 47xx No. 4707 on the up fast line at Goring and Streatley bound for Reading, where a pause will be made to change engines for the final leg to Victoria.

W. Gilburt

Manual labour at Cholsey and Wallingford, the staff moving the levers of the ground frame to allow access onto the former Wallingford branch for a special working in December 1966. By this time the former station signalbox, which had controlled the junction, was closed and the Wallingford branch being used for goods only was classified as a siding. Accordingly Reading MAS panel would give an electric release to the Annett's key which would in turn unlock the ground frame.

J. Fairman

Wallingford terminus, 6.9.58. Auto trains with a 14xx and a single coach were the usual method of operating the 2½ mile branch from Cholsey and although apparently devoid of passengers on this occasion the line retained a good patronage during the morning and evening peaks. In addition there was private siding traffic from a dairy and maltsters premises both of which finally ceased in 1981. Today a preservation society is attempting to resurrect part of the route but the station itself has been lost to redevelopment. During the 1970's BR had used the line for the temporary stabling of the new HST sets, as for much of its course it was on a shallow embankment ideal for making publicity photographs.

Tony Bennett

Footplate crews learnt their trade first through the shunting and goods grades before eventually progressing to the passenger links and finally top line duties. After all if the man could handle a heavy, loose coupled freight with little braking power he had an excellent grounding for passenger services later. The crew of No. 9073 *Mounts Bay* could expect several years of this type of work as they work a train of empties west of Cholsey in 1948. Despite the shocking appearance of the engine it would at least appear to be steaming well with a 'white feather' from the safety valves.

Roger Sherlock

To the passenger it may well have been just the railway between London and Bristol, but from the drivers there was perhaps a better description, 'Brunel's billiard table', a tribute to the great Victorian engineer who originally laid out the first Great Western Railway. On the racing ground between Reading and Didcot, No. 5030 *Shirburn Castle* crosses the Thames near Cholsey with the 1.55 p.m. down, Paddington–South Wales express on 8.4.50.

J.F. Russell Smith/National Railway Museum

Relaying the permanent way near Cholsey in 1961. The first stage was to relay the line with concrete sleeper sections in 60ft. lengths. While this settles, new continous welded rails have previously been unloaded either side of the existing track. Next the fittings were removed from the short sections and then with the aid of a drawn machine the old rails are replaced by the long welded rail.

'R. A.' Collection

An immaculate No. 5099 *Compton Castle* at the head of the London bound 'Red Dragon' express from South Wales near Moreton, east of Didcot in September 1951. Shortly after this 'Britannia' engines were substituted on the duty, the standard type allocated to Cardiff Canton shed. The South Wales men were some of the few 'Western crews to take to the 'Pacific' type.

J.F. Russell Smith/National Railway Museum

Fifty three 'Dean Goods' engines survived into nationalisation and were still employed on the type of duty for which they had been introduced way back in 1883. No. 2532 is at the head of a 50 wagon train near Moreton, bound for Reading in the early years of BR ownership. The engine is attached to a small tender of just 2500 gallons water capacity and it is also interesting to note the first three vehicles are tank cars without any form of barrier separating them from the locomotive.

Collection of P. T. Earl

The exterior of Didcot station as it appeared until recently when the passenger accommodation was extensively rebuilt. Access to the platforms was via a subway extending beneath all the main lines and also used by men going to work at the loco shed. The booking office was just inside the subway entrance and was a dismal affair that required the use of artificial light throughout the day.

'R. A.' Collection

One of the Didcot shed's Hall's, No. 6937 *Conyngham Hall* shunting parcel vans in the station during December 1963. This may well have been part of the seasonal peak of Post Office traffic as a number of mail bags can be seen on the platform alongside the engine. In the right background it is just possible to catch a glimpse of the engine shed. Although in the photograph the weather would appear to be mild, Didcot station has often been referred to as the coldest place at which to wait when forced to change trains.

'M.N.L.P.S.'

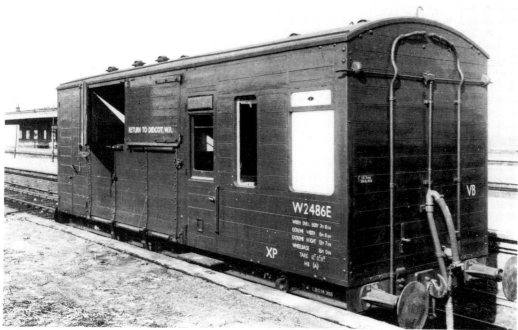

Other than its importance as a junction, Didcot was really little more than a village that developed into a town as a consequence of the arrival of the railway. Indeed there were just two main areas of employment, agriculture and the railway. Existing as it did in a mainly rural community, the station handled an amount of local traffic including the transport of racehorses. These were often brought to the station from a wide area, many from as far as Lambourn, as by doing so the trainers could reduce the time and cost of rail transport via Newbury and similarly Didcot was better suited for direct access to the lines to the north and west.

'R.A.' Collection

A brand new Hawksworth 'County', fresh out of Swindon works arriving at Didcot on a running-in turn. No. 1018 *County of Leicester* will spend some little while on such duties before being allocated to one of the main depôts. In the background a train of coal empties is passing on the east curve with several of the wagons showing their origins as private owner vehicles.

Collection of P.T. Earl

Didcot was also the junction for the main line to the north with a triangle formed between the Bristol and Oxford lines. Within the triangle was a shunting yard and extensive sidings and also the locomotive shed which had replaced a smaller wooden affair back in 1932. Still sporting its GWR livery, No. 1335 stands outside the front of the shed with its ATC shoe gear visible under the front buffer beam.

Collection of P.T. Earl

Towards the end of its life as a steam shed, Didcot depôt also played host to a number of diesel types even if the servicing conditions were far from ideal for their delicate engine components. Three 350 h.p shunters are visible, the rear of each cab painted in the 'waspish' black and yellow stripes intended as a warning to men working near the trackside.

J. Fairman

Almost the end at Didcot with No. 7929 being coaled in the time honoured way by tub. The engine had formally carried the name *Wyke Hall* and yet here is devoid of even its cabside number. Coaling plant men were often paid on piecework rates and hence would load every engine to its limit. The 'Western mostly used soft Welsh coal which provided a fierce heat from a smaller area but was unsuitable for delivery by means of the hopper coal plants seen on other regions.

J. Fairman

The shed was officially closed to steam in June 1965 and by this time conditions were decidedly run down both from the point of view of maintainance facilities as well as the engines themselves. With just a few weeks to go, Nos. 7829, 6969 & 6953 present a dejected appearance outside the depôt.

J. Fairman

No. 6918 alongside the locomens cabin and offices at Didcot shed.

Roger Sherlock

Eastleigh crews who ventured to Didcot found conditions at the shed there very different from what they had perhaps previously imagined the 'Western to be. Neither was this the time to voice comment on such differences as with a variety of 'Western men from as far afield as South Wales, Wolverhampton, Old Oak and Westbury, those loyal to the GWR outnumbered their critics by perhaps 20 to 1. Accordingly such comments as the B.H.O.B. (blower-hard-on-brigade) were discreetly not mentioned against a background hub of conversation on the relative prowess of one particular 'Castle' against another.

Slowly though the foreman would find tasks for the 'Western crews until perhaps with only two or three crews left the general atmosphere became more congenial and to which the Eastleigh crew could at last join in. 'Have some tea lads, plenty of it', remarked a driver and the Southern men glad of this opportunity to talk at last gladly agreed. Several cups later the ice was well and truely broken. '. . . my old Dad worked the Newbury line years back . . .', remarked a broad Berkshire voice, 'here look at this . . .', and rumaging in his pocket produced a faded and cracked photograph of his father on a 'Dean Goods' somewhere on the branch. There before your very eyes was the image of the driver of yesteryear. Tall, erect and with a cap screwed on his head as only a GWR hat could be – some say those caps were fitted at Swindon.

Whilst this was going on Samantha the shed cat had crept into the cabin and ever being in search of a tasty morsel would wander from driver to fireman to beg, cajole or even steal a piece of ham, corned beef or spam. Some would persuade her to stay awhile although those in the know discreetly pushed her away, but it was not so obvious to the two Eastleigh men.

Eventually the Southern crew were the only ones remaining and Samantha had curled up

125

happily on a big greasy set of overalls. Came the time for departure neither man could understand why the foreman suddenly burst out laughing as he came to tell them the train they were to relieve on had at last arrived. All was revealed though not long after departure, for Samantha had left them a present. She was the most flea and mite infested feline for miles around and amidst the warmth of the footplate most of the little varmits were coming to life. 'B. . . . Western men remarked the driver . . .', trying to decide whether opening the regulator a bit more or satisfying the latest itch should have priority. The fireman did not reply, he was contemplating diving into the tender tank in an effort to find some relief, but thought better of it for the moment at least.

In addition there were the first signs of 'Didcot gyp', a strange stomach complaint caused by over indulgence in tea produced from a none too clean pot belied stove within the locomens cabin. The Southern men would remember Didcot, and remember it well, but there was time before the next visit and perhaps the opprotunity to think of revenge. . . .

Hugh Abbinnett

Towards the very end of steam there was little variety compared with the numerous types that had existed only a few years earlier. The Hall's lasted right to the bitter end with No. 6953 showing signs of neglect outside the front of Didcot depôt early in 1965. Fortunately compared with most other steam sheds which were razed to the ground Didcot has survived as the home of the Great Western Society.

Roger Sherlock

Temporarily provided with a small set of rear wheels, No. 9773 stands out of use in the 'field' alongside Didcot shed. The proper rear driving wheels were no doubt in for repair, although in the last years even a routine defect was sufficient to warrant the withdrawal of an engine from service.

Roger Sherlock

14xx No. 1445 in store at Didcot early in 1963, for although many more years of servicable life were left there was no suitable work available. Notice the cover tied to the chimney and intended to prevent undue deterioration until the engine was needed to re-enter traffic. In practice few ever did.

Roger Sherlock

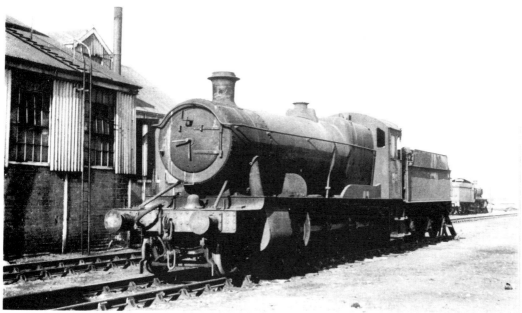

With coupling rods partly removed and devoid of numberplates, No. 3819 will not steam again. The engine is awaiting the final trip to the scrapyard as perhaps £2000 worth of metal. Didcot, 27.2.65.

J. Fairman

An unusual sight at Didcot was one of the heavy 15xx series of pannier tanks, and the only class of pannier to have outside valve gear. The short wheel base on these engines meant they were really only suitable for shunting duties and most spent their time on empty carriage workings between Paddington and the sidings at Old Oak. Just visible behind is No. 5742, which is fitted with a spark arrestor to the chimney so as to be able to work within the confines of Didcot Ordnance depôt.

Courtney Haydon

Inside the lifting shop at Didcot during BR days with a pannier tank receiving attention. Most of the larger running sheds possessed such facilities and were thus able to cope with normal lifting tasks such as that dictated when an axlebox or bearing needed attention.

J. Fairman

An impressive low angle view of No. 3866 on Didcot east curve and bound for Oxford. The young fireman is evidently glad of the chance of a breather. March 1965.

Roger Sherlock

The west side of the triangle at Didcot with No. 4912 *Berrington Hall* at the head of the Wolverhampton–Weymouth through working. The engine is attached to an 'intermediate' size tender with five of the six coaches apparently to differing designs.

Collection of P.T. Earl

SR Merchant Navy Pacific, No. 35011 *General Steam Navigation* bound for Oxford with the Bournemouth–York through service on Didcot east curve during early 1965. Peering from the window is Driver Lees of Eastleigh, who along with his fireman took over the train at Southampton. The crew worked to Oxford and returned to Southampton on a balanced working as their days duty.

Roger Sherlock

On 14.8.64, Stanier 8F No. 48734 was badly damaged in a fire when in charge of a petrol tanker train at Didcot. The engine was just leaving the north yard at the head of its train when the first two wagons jumped the rails in the course of which one of the following tank cars was punctured. Fire broke out almost at once and after heroic efforts to uncouple the rest of the train the crew had to abandon their engine. So intense was the heat that a nearby metal overbridge distorted, having the same effect upon the engine itself. One week later No. 48734 was at Didcot shed and not surprisingly was immediately withdrawn.

J. Fairman

Prior to the revision of county boundaries the railway both in Didcot, and for some few miles north, came within the administrative area of Berkshire. 61xx No. 6152 working bunker first near Appleford with a mixed freight for Oxford in May 1964. At this time many of the 61xx class engines had already been withdrawn and the remainder were often to be found on menial duties as an alternative to the passenger turns once handled.

Les Elsey

Disaster at Appleford level-crossing on 25.9.52 when No. 7311 over-ran the loop points and collided end on with the signalbox which was totally demolished. The force of the accident was sufficient to slew both the loop and main lines badly out of true, the permanent way gang posed for the camera prior to commencing work on the damaged track.

'R.A.' Collection

Seen from the other side this was the scene before the breakdown gangs had cleared away the main line and as seems usual for an accident it was attracting a wide variety of attention.

'R.A.' Collection

Besides the obvious debris scattered around, Appleford signalbox was totally demolished in the impact, the steel lever frame twisted like matchwood and now naked and unprotected amidst the timber and brick rubble. The 'box was later rebuilt in almost exactly its original style with a view of the reconstruction shown in the earlier volume *Last Days of Steam in Oxfordshire*.

'R.A.' Collection

Often employed on similar duties to the larger 'Hall' class engines the 2-6-0 43xx class were true maids of all work although with a reputation for the occasional voracious appetite for coal when loaded to their limit. One of the later series, No. 6381 is at the head of a through freight at Appleford bound for Didcot.

'R.A.' Collection

Appleford again but this time with a 'Hall' on a similar duty. No. 7909 *Heveningham Hall* on a Didcot–Hinksey working in May 1964. For the period the engine is remarkably clean and still retains its nameplates.

Tony Molyneaux

Our final look at steam in Berkshire begins west of Didcot and the line to Swindon. Steventon has already been referred to briefly in the Oxfordshire volume, but here is a glimpse at the open country near the station and with a rare bird in the form of 56xx 0-6-2T No. 5629 at the head of a down freight. Most of the engines of this type spent their working lives on the movement of coal trains in the valleys of Wales with the design being a direct descendant from a number of similar types inherited by the GWR at the grouping of 1923.

Collection of P.T. Earl

Throughout almost the whole of its independant existance the GWR had an enviable safety record for the conveyance of passengers, so much so that the safety aspects of the old company were commented upon a number of times by the Railway Inspectorate when it came to the investigation of accidents on other lines. Unfortunately such a charmed existence came to a sudden end at Milton, west of Didcot on Sunday 20.11.55, when at 1.13 p.m. 'Britannia' Class Pacific, No. 70026 *Polar Star* at the head of an excursion from Treherbert to Paddington was derailed at the entrance to the goods loop and fell some feet down the nearby embankment with the coaches piling up behind. Eleven passengers were killed and 163 other persons injured. It was soon clear that the cause of the accident was excess speed. The train signalled to cross onto the goods loop as its normal passage along the main line was impeded by engineering works. On the same day several other passenger trains had already accomplished this manouever without incident. At the resultant enquiry blame was primarily apportioned on the driver, although several other railway employees were also criticised to varying degrees with the design of the engine also coming under close scrutiny. It transpired that complaints had previously been made by drivers over the view of signals from these engines which were left hand drive compared with the right hand drive Western machines. (Signals on the WR were also positioned for optimum viewing from the right hand side.) The hand rail on the smoke deflectors came in for particular comment as this could obscure the already poor forward vision still further. As a result of the enquiry a series of tests were made with an engine of the same type and so positioned as to repeat the indication the driver of the ill-fated train would have had as he approached the divergence. This first view then is from the drivers side approaching Milton and with the signal to indicate a turn into the loop in the 'off' position.

British Railways

139

No. 70026 came to rest on its side at the foot of the embankment and whilst recovery of the tender and coaches could be accomplished by crane, movement of the 94 ton locomotive was another matter, especially as to reach the scene a crane would have to swing out some distance from the nearest rails with a corresponding reduction in lift capacity. Fortunately for the recovery teams an alternative existed with the close proximity of the rail complex within the Didcot Ordnance Depôt. By extending a siding from there it was possible to haul the locomotive out once it had been brought upright. With an old engine the decision may well have been to cut it up on site but No. 70026 was less than three years old at the time. Accordingly the same arrangement was used to right *Polar Star* as had been used at Shawford (SR) in 1952, meaning the ground was dug away both underneath and to the side of the engine and replaced with a bed of sleepers. Rails were then attached to the wheels of the engine and by means of a system of jacks and winches she was restored to an even keel. No. 70026 seen still partly buried in the soft ground but with the early stages of righting work in progress.

British Railways

The prepared sleeper bed with rails attached to the underside of the driving wheels. A good comparison as to size is available from the men stood on top of the embankment by the side of the Milton up loop.

British Railways

Sunday 4 December and the eventual recovery of *Polar Star*. As each stage is completed the men on the far right will add packing to prevent the engine slipping back whilst the 92 ton bulk of 2-8-2T No. 7239 is being used to stabilise the embankment whilst lifting takes place.

British Railways

The engine was subsequently towed away from the site through the Ordnance Depôt by a 22xx, and on very temporary track indeed. No. 70026 was later repaired at Swindon and saw several further years service on the 'Western and later Midland regions. A direct consequence of this accident was that the handrails were removed from the smoke deflectors of the engines in the class and replaced by grab holes.

British Railways

Normal working is resumed, with another engine type of which few examples lasted into BR days. This is an 'Aberdare' 2-6-0, No. 2651 from the look of which had not long to go judging by the steam leakage from the inside cylinders and glands. Most crews loathed these engines for a variety of reasons, one of the few 'Western types to be so despised. The engine is seen west of Milton on a down train with a glum looking fireman peering round the side of the cab.

Collection of P.T. Earl

'Saint' class 4-6-0, No. 2949 *Stanford Court* paused at Wantage Road with an up stopper in April 1950. As with the 'Bulldog's' and 'Duke's' then confined to freight working, so by this time the 'Saint's' and 'Star's' were relegated to local and stopping passenger work although the speedometer drive attached to the rear driving wheel is perhaps an indication of past glories. These engines with their 6ft. 8½in. driving wheels were flyers in every sense of the word although there was little opportunity for high speed on the type of working shown here. Years earlier one of the class was credited with an unofficial GWR speed record of 120 mph when running light west of Swindon, but without verification the truth can now never be known.

Collection of P.T. Earl

Passing a decidedly shabby signalbox at Wantage Road is a 'Warship' diesel on a Paddington bound express. Wantage Road had originally been the connecting station with the standard gauge tramway to the town of the same name, although when this view was taken in May 1964 the trams had ceased running some years back. The station too did not have long to go as it was closed in May 1965 in the same decade as all the other intermediate stopping places between Swindon and Didcot. There was hope at one time of a modern 'Parkway' station to serve the growing community nearby but this was rejected in favour of developing Didcot a few miles further east.

Les Elsey

On the duty for which it was intended, No. 4703 at the head of a heavy through freight near Wantage Road in September 1951. Today it is hard to imagine when such sights were an every day occurance, so much so that people would ignore the humble freight in favour of the more glamorous passenger train with perhaps a 'Castle' or 'King' at its head. But oh for a chance to return to this the scene of yesterday, a glorious late summer day spent recording trains from the lineside, there were few more pleasurable experiences.

T.E. Williams/National Railway Museum

With a number of new sleepers by the linside ready for relaying, a 93xx series 'Mogul' makes steady progress westwards with an afternoon freight near Challow in November 1948.

Collection of P. T. Earl

Regular milk trains are now a thing of the past although a line of tank cars for this type of traffic is still retained in servicable condition at Swindon in the event of a sudden shortage perhaps caused by drought. No. 5958 *Knolton Hall* is at the head of an empty train of milk tanks on the down line at Challow in April 1959. In charge of the train are three men, driver, fireman and guard and yet in equivalent terms perhaps 20 road tankers and their drivers are required to move the same load in the 1980's. Even to the anti-railway protagonist this must surely be a matter of lost priorities.

Tony Bennett

As with the steam engine so many branch lines are now but a memory. This is one of the original Berkshire lines now long gone, the three mile line to Faringdon from Uffington which closed to all traffic in July 1963. 0-6-0 saddle tank No. 1363, of a type more usually found shunting the quay lines at Plymouth or Weymouth, is at the head of a two coach special train organised by the 'Railway Enthusiasts Club' from Farnborough (Hants), depicted at the station on 26.4.59.

Hugh Davies

A final pause to reflect upon a scene once commonplace and for which so many of us still long – perhaps as a means of escape from the technology orientated lifestyle of today. The steam engine and the branch line, the final link on a journey begun amidst the bustle of the main line station. This was East Garston with a Lambourn train departing, we can but wish to be on it. . . .

R. Denison